MAXnotes®

D0112953

Albert Camus'

The Stranger

Text by
Kevin Kelly
(M.F.A., Columbia University)
Department of Communications
Andover College
Portland, Maine

Illustrations by
Karen Pica

 Research & Education Association

What **MAXnotes**® Will Do for You

This book is intended to help you absorb the essential contents and features of Albert Camus' *The Stranger* and to help you gain a thorough understanding of the work. The book has been designed to do this more quickly and effectively than any other study guide.

For best results, this **MAXnotes** book should be used as a companion to the actual work, not instead of it. The interaction between the two will greatly benefit you.

To help you in your studies, this book presents the most up-to-date interpretations of every section of the actual work, followed by questions and fully explained answers that will enable you to analyze the material critically. The questions also will help you to test your understanding of the work and will prepare you for discussions and exams.

Meaningful illustrations are included to further enhance your understanding and enjoyment of the literary work. The illustrations are designed to place you into the mood and spirit of the work's settings.

The **MAXnotes** also include summaries, character lists, explanations of plot, and section-by-section analyses. A biography of the author and discussion of the work's historical context will help you put this literary piece into the proper perspective of what is taking place.

The use of this study guide will save you the hours of preparation time that would ordinarily be required to arrive at a complete grasp of this work of literature. You will be well prepared for classroom discussions, homework, and exams. The guidelines that are included for writing papers and reports on various topics will prepare you for any added work which may be assigned.

The **MAXnotes** will take your grades "to the max."

Dr. Max Fogiel
Program Director

Contents

Section One: *Introduction* 1

   The Life and Work of Albert Camus 1

   Historical Background 3

   Master List of Characters 5

   Summary of the Novel 7

   Estimated Reading Time 9

Each Chapter includes List of Characters, Summary, Analysis, Study Questions and Answers, and Suggested Essay Topics.

Section Two: *Part One* 10

   Chapter 1 10

   Chapter 2 16

   Chapter 3 21

   Chapter 4 27

Chapter 5 33
Chapter 6 39

Section Three: *Part Two* 47
Chapter 1 47
Chapter 2 54
Chapter 3 61
Chapter 4 68
Chapter 5 73

Section Four: *Sample Analytical Paper Topics* 79

Section Five: *Bibliography* 85

SECTION ONE

Introduction

The Life and Work of Albert Camus

Albert Camus was born in Monrovia, Algeria on November 7, 1913. His father, a soldier in World War I, died fighting for France during the first Battle of Marne in 1914. Although Camus never really knew his father, while he was growing up, and later as an adult, Camus was keenly aware of the circumstances of his father's death. At an early age Camus was made painfully aware of the tragic effects of war, experiencing the consequences of political strife on a highly personal level.

Following the publication of *The Stranger* and several other important works, Albert Camus gained wide recognition as one of the leading French writers of his day. As he continued to produce critically acclaimed and controversial novels, plays, and essays, Camus would earn a reputation equal to other preeminent French authors of the time such as Simone de Beauvoir, Jean-Paul Sartre, and Andre Malraux. Camus' work had a significant and lasting influence on a post-war generation concerned with political and philosophical issues that dealt with human alienation and the search for meaning in a troubled world.

After his father's death, Camus, his mother, and older brother moved to Belcourt, a suburb of Algiers where they lived in poverty for many years. In 1930, while a high school student, Camus contracted tuberculosis and barely survived. When he recovered, Camus' excellent grades in school helped get him admitted to the University of Algiers where he studied theater and wrote plays, essays, and fiction. Camus' illness, however, was another significant event in his life and it gave him a new perspective on death and awareness of his own existence. While he also began to develop the political outlook and personal philosophy that would form the basis of all of his later work, the inevitability of death would become an important theme in Camus' work, one he would explore in much of his writing.

While he was attending the University of Algiers, Camus supported himself by working at a number of odd, part-time jobs, including one with the French Algerian civil service where he processed auto registrations and driver's licenses. This dull, routine job made an impression on Camus; later he would incorporate elements of the experience in his writing of *The Stranger*.

In 1937, Camus' first book *The Wrong Side and the Right Side* (*L'Envers et l'endroit*) was published in Algiers. It described his life growing up in Belcourt. In 1938, Camus was hired by *Alge-Republicain*, an anti-colonialist newspaper, where he took on a variety of editorial tasks, wrote literary reviews, covered local meetings, and wrote articles concerning the desperate conditions of impoverished Arabs living under French rule in Algeria. Of particular note was his description of the famine in Kabylia. In his article, Camus described the devastation within some Arab families where only two out of 10 children survived.

With the outbreak of World War II, Camus joined an underground anti-Nazi group based in Paris and became editor of the group's resistance newspaper *Combat*. It was during this time that Camus wrote some of his most important work, including *The Stranger* (1942), and developed his theory of the absurd, which declared that life is essentially meaningless because of the inevitability of death. Camus, however, was never satisfied with the absurdist attitude of moral indifference. His experiences in occupied France, and other political events he witnessed, caused him to develop opinions on moral responsibility. Some of these ideas are contained in his *Letters to a German Friend* (1945), and in the essays included in *Resistance, Rebellion, and Death* (1960).

The Stranger is a striking example of Camus' belief that "a novel is a philosophy put into images." He believed that the highest art should contain elements of diversity and complexity, while maintaining a style that is balanced, uniform, and straightforward. Sartre immediately recognized the existential quality of *The Stranger*, although his opinion about the novel and its relation to existentialism would later prove to be controversial.

Other works by Camus that explore his philosophical and political ideas include *Caligula* (1944); *The Plague* (1947), a novel; the long, controversial essay, *The Rebel* (1951); and a third novel, *The Fall* published in 1957. His famous essay *The Myth of Sisyphus*, published in 1942, concerns Sisyphus, a Greek mythological figure who was condemned by the gods to spend an eternal, meaningless existence pushing a huge boulder up and over a hill, and then back again from the other side.

Following the publication of *The Fall*, Camus was awarded the Nobel Prize for Literature in 1957. During his career, Camus became well known for his political views and activism. Although an anti-communist, he was an outspoken critic of capitalism, and he remained a proponent of democratic socialism and nonviolent confrontation. He believed in the principle of *le juste milieu* which recognized that the solution to human problems is not usually found in absolute strategies or ideas.

In 1960, Camus died suddenly in an automobile accident. Camus' work, and the political, religious, and ethical issues it deals with, remains controversial, but his writing endures because it expresses Camus' profound concern for human suffering and the philosophical and moral dilemmas faced by all individuals.

Historical Background

The Stranger takes place in Algiers, the capital of Algeria, a North African country located along the Mediterranean Sea. (Algiers is a port city, and the many ships that dock there bring a broad mix of people from other countries to the bustling city.) Also, because of its close proximity to Europe, the area known today as Algeria has had contact with other cultures for centuries. In 1942, when *The Stranger* was published, Algeria had been a colonial possession of France for almost a hundred years. Arabs, Europeans, and pieds-noirs—people of European descent born, as Camus was, in Algeria—all lived side by side in crowded Algiers. It was a situation that naturally gave rise to the tension and unrest that is reflected in *The Stranger*. The climate of North Africa, with its heat, sun, and beaches, also has a powerful influence on the events and characters in Camus' book.

In 1830, the French invaded Algeria and began to promote European colonization of the country. Settlers from Europe confiscated Muslim land, created a separate society, and imposed their own culture on the native population. France finally conquered the northern part of the country in 1847, and gradually extended its influence to the south despite fierce local resistance. More than a million European settlers—mostly French—owned the country's principal industrial, commercial, and agricultural enterprises. The majority of the 8.5 million Muslims had low paying jobs and often worked performing menial tasks for the Europeans. The native Muslim population had little political influence and lived in relative poverty compared to their wealthy colonial rulers.

The French created Algeria's current boundaries in 1902. While most of the people living in Algeria today are Arabs or Berbers, in the nineteenth century, Europeans comprised almost 10 percent of the total population. The European impact on Algeria was enormous, with large European-style cities standing alongside ancient villages and tiny farms.

By the early 1900s, economic conditions in Algeria began to decline steadily as its growing population became increasingly restless and resentful of foreign rule. In addition, World War I had a devastating effect on all of the countries in the region. The political and economic impact of the war was great, and the psychological repercussions were equally traumatic. New technology, developed in the war, had greatly expanded the military's ability to kill. The aftermath was horrendous. France alone lost over one million soldiers on the battlefield, with many more wounded and maimed. Adding to France's political troubles after the war ended, Algerian nationalist movements began to fight for independence against the French. European settlers, now firmly established in the country, bitterly resisted any efforts to grant political rights to the Algerians.

It was into this highly charged atmosphere of racial tension and political unrest that Albert Camus was born. He would spend the first half of his life in this uneasy and difficult environment. Camus' father had died fighting for France and Camus grew up acutely aware of the wholesale slaughter that took place during the war. By the time *The Stranger* was published, France and the world

Checked out item summary for
Pastran Fonesca, Camila Andrea
29-01-2011 11:15AM

BARCODE: 32104033797814
LOCATION: cej
TITLE: The Lion encyclopedia of world re
DUE DATE: 02-02-2011 **TOO MANY RENEWAL

BARCODE: 32104002586743
LOCATION: cej
TITLE: Cupid and Psyche : a love story /
DUE DATE: 19-02-2011 * RENEWED

BARCODE: 32104021694072
LOCATION: cej
TITLE: One world, many religions : the w
DUE DATE: 19-02-2011 * RENEWED

BARCODE: 32104026591901
LOCATION: cej
TITLE: Religions of the world / the edit
DUE DATE: 19-02-2011 * RENEWED

BARCODE: 32104035185372
LOCATION: bea
TITLE: Albert Camus' The stranger / text
DUE DATE: 19-02-2011 * RENEWED

BARCODE: 32104028821041
LOCATION: ceala
TITLE: La puerta de la misericordia / To
DUE DATE: 19-02-2011 * RENEWED

were engaged in another costly war, this time against Germany and the Axis powers. World War II was a conflict that would exact an enormous death toll and again have a significant influence on Camus' thinking. The certainty of death would become a major theme in all of his work.

With the publication of *The Stranger*, Camus received instant recognition for his achievement, although reaction to the book was controversial and opinions were divided. Some, like Jean-Paul Sartre, would embrace its existential quality, while others considered it a political work addressing the problems of French colonialism in Algeria. Many critics felt the novel dealt with atheism and religion. In discussing Camus' writing style in *The Stranger*, Sartre noted that "each sentence is a present instant...sharp, distinct, and self-contained. It is separated by a void from the following one." Sartre goes on to explain his view of the philosophical significance of Camus' style: "The world is destroyed and reborn from sentence to sentence...We bounce from sentence to sentence, from void to void." Camus, however, would dispute much of what was said about his novel. Ultimately, *The Stranger* has become an enduring work of fiction because it is concerned not only with politics and racism, but also with universal philosophical themes and the basic dilemmas of the human condition.

Master List of Characters

Meursault—*The protagonist and narrator of* The Stranger.

Employer—*Meursault's boss and owner of the business where Meursault works.*

Celeste—*Meursault's friend and the proprietor of Meursault's favorite neighborhood restaurant.*

Doorkeeper—*A small, older man who works at the Home where Meursault's mother lived. He sits with Meursault and helps keep an all-night vigil over the mother's body.*

Old Women—*A group of elderly women who live at the Home and also keep vigil over the mother's body.*

Warden—*The director of the Home who helps Meursault with his mother's funeral.*

Thomas Perez—*Meursault's mother's "special friend" at the Home who attends her funeral with Meursault.*

Marie Cardona—*A former typist at Meursault's office who begins an affair with Meursault the day after his mother's funeral.*

Emmanuel—*A young man, and friend of Meursault's, who works in the Forwarding Department of Meursault's office.*

Old Salamano—*A sad, cantankerous old man who lives with his mangy, mistreated dog in Meursault's building.*

Raymond Sintes—*A tough, young warehouse worker, and possibly a pimp, who abuses his girlfriend. He lives in Meursault's building and becomes Meursault's friend.*

Raymond's Girlfriend—*A young Arab woman who is beaten by Raymond.*

Policeman—*An irate police officer who reprimands and strikes Raymond for beating his girlfriend.*

Robot Woman—*An odd little woman who sits at Meursault's table at Celeste's.*

The Arab—*Raymond's girlfriend's brother who follows Raymond, Meursault, and Marie to the beach.*

Second Arab—*The Arab's companion who helps the Arab fight Raymond and Masson on the beach.*

Masson—*Raymond's slow-talking friend who owns a small bungalow on the beach.*

Mme. Masson—*Masson's wife, a "plump, cheerful little woman" who likes Meursault and Marie.*

Examining Magistrate—*A serious man who questions Meursault about the crime after Meursault's arrest.*

The Lawyer—*Meursault's young, court-appointed defense attorney.*

Chief Jailer—*A friendly prison guard who is kind to Meursault.*

Court Policeman—*One of the officers who guards Meursault during his trial.*

The Journalist—*One of several reporters who is covering Meursault's trial. He informs Meursault that his case is being covered by a newspaper in Paris.*

The Public Prosecutor—*A tall, thin man in a red gown who aggressively seeks a conviction and death sentence during Meursault's trial.*

The Judge—*The chief justice who presides over the trial and questions Meursault on the witness stand about the crime.*

Chaplain—*A priest who visits Meursault in prison after his conviction and tries to convince Meursault of the existence of God.*

Summary of the Novel

In Part One, Meursault works as a shipping clerk in Algiers, a city in North Africa. He learns of his mother's death, and although he is somewhat ambivalent upon hearing the news, he travels to the nursing home to attend her funeral and sit in vigil over her body. At the funeral he displays little emotion and is not interested in viewing his mother's body.

The following day, back in Algiers, Meursault meets a young woman, Marie Cardona, and they go swimming together. Because of Meursault's cheerful attitude, Marie is surprised to learn of his mother's death. Later, in the evening, they see a comic film together and then return to Meursault's apartment where they make love. Meursault spends the next day alone in his apartment, eating, and watching people pass by on the street.

The following evening, Raymond Sintes, a neighbor with a shady background, invites Meursault to his apartment for dinner. Although he doesn't really know Meursault, Raymond asks him to write a nasty letter to his Arab girlfriend. Raymond suspects his girlfriend of seeing other men. For no particular reason, Meursault agrees to help him.

Meursault and Marie go to the beach again the next Saturday. That night they hear Raymond beating his girlfriend in his apartment. A policeman arrives and rebukes Raymond for hitting the young woman. The policeman smacks Raymond around and orders him to appear in court. Although Marie is upset over the incident, Meursault tells Raymond he will testify on his behalf.

The following Sunday, Meursault and Marie go to the beach with Raymond. At the bus stop, Raymond points out two Arab men who are following him. He tells them that one of the Arabs is the brother of his ex-girlfriend.

At the beach, Meursault and Marie meet Raymond's friend Masson and Masson's wife. Masson owns a cottage on the beach and the three men discuss spending the month of August there together. Later, Meursault, Raymond, and Masson walk on the beach and meet the two Arabs who have followed them from the city. The men fight and one Arab cuts Raymond with a knife before running off. After his cuts are treated, Raymond takes a revolver and searches for the Arabs. Meursault follows him and talks him out of using the gun when they again meet up with the Arabs. Meursault takes Raymond's gun and puts it in his pocket.

Meursault and Raymond return to Masson's beach house. Meursault walks on the beach by himself, experiencing the hot, muggy weather. Meursault wanders towards a cool stream where he meets the Arab again. With the blinding sun in his eyes, Meursault confronts the Arab and shoots him with Raymond's gun.

In Part Two, Meursault spends almost a year in prison before his trial begins. He is interviewed many times by the examining magistrate and his own defense attorney. Meursault aggravates both men with his lack of remorse for the crime and his unfeeling attitude about his own mother's recent death. He angers the magistrate when he reveals that he does not believe in God. The magistrate becomes convinced that Meursault is a cold-hearted criminal.

Everyone Meursault knows testifies at his trial. His lawyer conducts a weak defense, and the prosecutor portrays Meursault as an unfeeling killer. When he takes the stand, Meursault can only say that "the sun" was the reason he shot the Arab. Meursault is found guilty and sentenced to death.

In his cell, awaiting his sentence, Meursault refuses to see the prison chaplain. The chaplain insists and finally gets in to see Meursault. He tries to convince Meursault of the existence of God and an afterlife, but Meursault rejects everything he hears and becomes enraged at the chaplain.

After the chaplain leaves, Meursault finds he is exhausted by his outburst, but he feels calm, appreciating the "marvelous peace" of the summer night. He describes a "benign" and "indifferent" universe where no one cares about his fate. The book ends with Meursault hoping that he is greeted with "howls of execration" by a huge, angry crowd on the day of his execution.

Estimated Reading Time

The average reader should be able to read *The Stranger* in four or five hours. The book could be read in one or two sessions. The novel is a quick read and is divided into two equal sections: Part One with six chapters, and Part Two with five chapters. The sentences are short and easy to understand and Camus' style is clear and distinct. The translation used here is by Stuart Gilbert and contains 154 pages.

SECTION TWO

Part One

Chapter 1

New Characters:

Meursault: *the narrator of the story*

The Employer: *Meursault's boss*

Celeste: *owner of Meursault's favorite restaurant*

Doorkeeper: *resident and employee of the nursing home*

Warden: *the director of the nursing home*

Old Women: *residents of the nursing home*

Thomas Perez: *Meursault's mother's "special friend"*

Summary

Meursault, a shipping clerk, lives in Algiers, a city in North Africa. He receives a telegram from a nursing home telling him that his mother has died. Meursault is somewhat interested in learning the details of her death but does not feel especially saddened by the news. His employer is annoyed that Meursault must take time off from work to attend the funeral. Meursault explains that it isn't his fault and is annoyed that his employer isn't more sympathetic. Meursault is concerned that his employer will blame him for leaving work and taking an extra long weekend.

After he leaves his office, Meursault eats lunch at his friend Celeste's restaurant, then takes a bus to the nursing home. He sleeps on the bus and is bothered by the sun glaring off the roadway.

At the nursing home he meets the doorkeeper who introduces him to the warden. The warden tells Meursault he shouldn't feel guilty for putting his mother in the home, but Meursault thinks the warden is blaming him. The warden shows Meursault where his mother's coffin is and leaves him alone with the body.

The doorkeeper arrives and starts to remove the lid of the coffin. Meursault tells him not to remove the lid because it doesn't matter if he sees his mother's body. The doorkeeper is surprised at this but he goes along with Meursault's request. Meursault chats with the doorkeeper who eventually brings him a cup of *cafe au lait*. They drink coffee and continue talking as they sit in front of the coffin.

During the all-night vigil, Meursault falls asleep in his chair. He complains of exhaustion and aching legs and is sensitive to the light in the room. Several elderly women enter the mortuary to attend the vigil. They do not speak to Meursault. One woman weeps. According to the doorkeeper, this woman was the mother's best friend; now she'll be all alone. As the sun rises, the vigil ends. Everyone shakes hands with Meursault and leaves. Meursault is hot and uncomfortable and he's glad the vigil is over.

The funeral procession begins, and Meursault sees Thomas Perez, a little old man described as his mother's "special friend." Meursault studies the old man's appearance and watches him take a series of shortcuts through town in order to keep up with the funeral party.

At the funeral, Meursault's senses are assaulted by the heat and the smell of horse dung and incense. He notices Perez crying during the funeral and recalls that at one point during the ceremony, Perez actually fainted. However, Meursault is tired and has a headache and appears to have little interest in the funeral. He is anxious for the proceeding to end so that he can return to his apartment in Algiers.

Analysis

Meursault responds primarily to the physical world around him. He reveals little about himself and his emotions, but he reacts strongly to environmental sensations such as the glare of the sun and the heat. In fact, his reaction to his environment is far more intense than any emotional feeling he displays over his mother's death.

Although he chats with the doorkeeper during the all-night vigil, Meursault makes no attempt to sympathize with the old women who are mourning his mother's passing. Meursault's reaction stands out in sharp contrast to the old women who are weeping over the loss of his mother. Meursault is interested in observing Thomas Perez, his mother's "special friend," but shows little concern over the old man's obvious grief. He shakes hands with Perez, but does nothing else to comfort him.

While society may expect Meursault to behave in a certain way, Meursault acts according to his own feelings and remains true to himself. Meursault's somewhat emotionless behavior and apparent indifference toward the vigil and funeral will play an important role in how society views him later on in the story.

Study Questions

1. Where does Meursault live?

2. How does Meursault react when he learns of his mother's death?

3. What happens when Meursault asks his employer for time off to attend his mother's funeral?

4. Who is Celeste?

5. What happens to Meursault on the bus to the nursing home?

6. How does Meursault feel when he talks to the warden?

7. What do Meursault and the doorkeeper do during the all-night vigil?

8. Who is Thomas Perez?

9. Does Meursault cry at his mother's funeral?

10. What does Meursault react to during the funeral?

Answers

1. Meursault, the narrator of the story, lives in Algiers, a hot, sun-drenched city in North Africa.

2. Meursault does not show any real emotion when he receives a telegram informing him of his mother's death; he only expresses a passing interest in the details.

3. The employer is somewhat irritated that Meursault will be away from the office. Meursault feels guilty at first, then annoyed that his employer is not more sympathetic.

4. Celeste is Meursault's friend and the owner of Meursault's favorite restaurant.

5. Meursault is bothered by the glaring sun on the road. He falls asleep during the ride.

6. Meursault feels uneasy and gets the impression that the warden blames him for putting his mother in the nursing home.

7. Meursault and the doorkeeper chat and drink *cafe au lait*. Meursault has a difficult time staying awake.

8. Thomas Perez is an old man who was Meursault's mother's "special friend." He cries and faints at the funeral.

9. No, Meursault does not cry or show any sadness, but he is anxious for the event to be over.

10. Meursault remains primarily concerned with his physical surroundings. He studies Perez's face, notices the heat and various odors around him, and observes the other graves in the cemetery and the color of the flowers.

Suggested Essay Topics

1. Discuss how Meursault responds to his natural surroundings, especially the sun and heat.

2. Discuss Meursault's feelings towards his mother when she was alive and his response when he learns of her death.

3. How do Meursault's reactions to death and the grief of others differ from what society generally considers appropriate behavior?

Chapter 2

New Character:

Marie Cardona: *a former typist at Meursault's office*

Summary

On Saturday, the day after his mother's funeral, Meursault wakes up feeling exhausted from his trip to the nursing home. He decides to go swimming, and at the local pool he meets Marie Cardona, a young woman who used to work at Meursault's office. Meursault and Marie enjoy swimming together and playing in the water. Meursault is attracted to Marie. He falls asleep on a raft, his head resting on her lap.

Later, Meursault asks Marie to go to a movie with him. They agree to see a comedy starring Fernandel, a French actor. Marie notices Meursault's black tie, and he casually mentions that his mother just died. Marie seems a bit unsettled by Meursault's lack of emotion.

That evening, Meursault and Marie go to the film. Afterwards, they return to his apartment and spend the night together.

When Meursault wakes up on Sunday morning, he discovers that Marie has already left. He sniffs at his pillow and recalls the scent of Marie's hair. Alone in bed, Meursault admits to himself that he has never enjoyed Sundays. He stays in bed until noon, smoking cigarettes. When he rises, he roams around his apartment somewhat aimlessly, looking for something to do.

From his bedroom window, Meursault observes the street scene below. He sees a family out for a Sunday walk and group of slick young men heading to the movies. He watches a tobacconist sitting on a chair outside his store, and a cafe waiter sweeping up sawdust.

Gradually, as the sun sets, the street becomes more crowded. Meursault watches the streetlights come on and observes the changing color of the sky. Finally, Meursault decides to make himself dinner, noting that somehow he's gotten through another Sunday, and that even though his mother just died, nothing in his life had really changed.

Analysis

In this chapter, Meursault is again seen as an individual who reacts strongly to his physical surroundings. He relishes the experience of swimming, the feel of the cool water and warm air on his "exhausted" body. When he meets Marie, he enjoys the sensation of being close to her, and the smell of her hair on his pillow. He notices the changes of the natural light outside his window, and the sights and sounds of the busy street below.

A day after burying his mother, an event that most people would consider traumatic, Meursault resumes his usual routine as if nothing of great significance had occurred. He goes for a swim, takes in a movie, and begins a casual romance with a woman he just happens to meet. The black tie that he wears is the only indication that Meursault has suffered a loss. He mentions his mother's death to Marie almost as an afterthought, as if it were just another mundane event in his life.

During the two days following his mother's funeral, Meursault's primary concern appears to be with the trivial activities of daily life. He moves from one occurrence to the next without becoming overly involved in anything that happens to him. Although he has just spent the night with Marie, he isn't particularly interested in where she went when he wakes up in the morning, and he doesn't seem to care if he will see her again. At day's end, he notes that he has "gotten through another Sunday," an indication that he is relieved to be returning to his job and his routine, work life.

Study Questions

1. Why does Meursault worry about his employer when he wakes up on Saturday morning?

2. Who is Marie Cardona?

3. What kind of movie does Marie want to see?

4. How does Marie react when Meursault tells her about his mother?

5. Why does Meursault decide not to eat at Celeste's on Sunday?

6. What does Meursault do when he's alone in his apartment?

7. Who does Meursault see from his bedroom window?

8. How does the tobacconist sit on his chair?

9. What does the football fan say to Meursault?

10. How does Meursault feel about Sundays?

Answers

1. Meursault worries that his employer will be annoyed at him for taking two days off right before the weekend, even though it was for his mother's funeral. He's afraid the employer will think he's taken a four day holiday for himself.

2. Marie Cardona used to work as a typist at Meursault's office. He meets her at the swimming pool on Saturday and they see each other again that night.

3. Marie wants to see a comedy starring the French actor Fernandel.

4. Meursault notes that Marie "shrank away a little" when he told her about his mother.

5. Meursault does not eat at Celeste's because he doesn't want to be bothered by people asking him questions about his mother's death.

6. Meursault stays in bed until noon, then he rises, eats, cuts an ad out of a newspaper, and sits by his window looking down at the street scene below.

7. Meursault watches an assortment of people pass by on the street below his window.

8. The tobacconist sits astride his chair with his folded arms resting on the back. Watching from his bedroom window, Meursault sits on his chair the same way, imitating the man.

9. The football fan calls up to Meursault: "We licked them!" Meursault calls back "Good work!"

10. Meursault has never cared for Sundays. They disrupt the perfunctory routine of his day-to-day existence.

Suggested Essay Topics

1. After telling Marie about his mother's death, Meursault mentions feeling "a bit guilty" about it. Why does Meursault feel the need to explain himself to both his employer and Marie?

2. Describe the way Meursault spends his Sunday. Why does he seem so content doing almost nothing?

3. Meursault doesn't like Sundays because they disrupt his normal routine. Why do you think Meursault would be bothered by this?

Chapter 3

New Characters:

Emmanuel: *a young man who works at Meursault's office*

Old Salamano: *an old man who lives in Meursault's building*

Raymond Sintes: *a tough young man who lives in Meursault's building*

Summary

Meursault returns to work on Monday morning. His employer, acting more concerned now, asks Meursault if he feels all right and inquires about the funeral. He asks Meursault how old his mother was when she died, but Meursault doesn't know her exact age. Meursault finds it odd that his employer would care.

As he begins his work day, Meursault notes that he enjoys washing his hands at work, at least until the end of the day when the towel in the bathroom becomes too wet. Meursault dislikes the feel of the soaking wet towel.

At noon, Meursault and his friend Emmanuel go to lunch. They run down the street and jump onto the back of a truck, hitching a ride to Celeste's restaurant. After he eats, Meursault takes a nap back in his apartment and later goes back to work.

That evening, Meursault walks home from the office, enjoying the cool night air. In the hallway of his building he meets Salamano, who is going out to walk his poor, miserable dog. Salamano

constantly complains about the dog. He always yells at his dog and beats him, especially when the dog charges ahead on the leash.

Another neighbor, Raymond Sintes, also meets Meursault in the hallway. Raymond, a tough young man, claims to be a warehouse worker, although Meursault has heard that he's a pimp. Raymond invites Meursault to his room for dinner and, having nothing better to do, Meursault accepts the invitation.

Raymond, whose hand is bandaged, tells Meursault that he had a fight with his girlfriend's brother. Raymond suspects his girlfriend of being unfaithful to him. He beat her up once, but he still wants revenge. He asks Meursault for advice, but Meursault tells him he wouldn't know what to do in such a situation.

Raymond thinks he should write his girlfriend a letter that will make her feel sorry for what she did to him. He believes this will encourage her to come back to him and then he can throw her out again. Raymond asks Meursault to write the letter.

Meursault writes the letter and Raymond is pleased. Now he considers Meursault his "pal." Meursault seems rather surprised at Raymond's sudden display of friendship, even though he's just done him a favor.

Raymond tells Meursault that he's sorry to hear of his mother's death, but, he adds, death is something that is "bound to happen one day or another." Meursault leaves Raymond's apartment and stands in the hallway for a moment, feeling the blood throbbing in his ears, and listening to old Salamano's dog moan.

Analysis

Meursault again fully experiences simple physical sensations such as washing his hands and the cool night air on his skin. Other matters are less important. His mother's age appears to be of little concern to him, but he is very interested in the wet towel in the bathroom. Although Meursault spends an entire day at work, he never really describes his job, concentrating instead on the trivial details that make up his daily routine. He remains detached, almost uninterested, in the events that most people would find meaningful and significant.

Meursault displays this same demeanor while considering Salamano's abuse of his dog, and the mistreatment of Raymond's

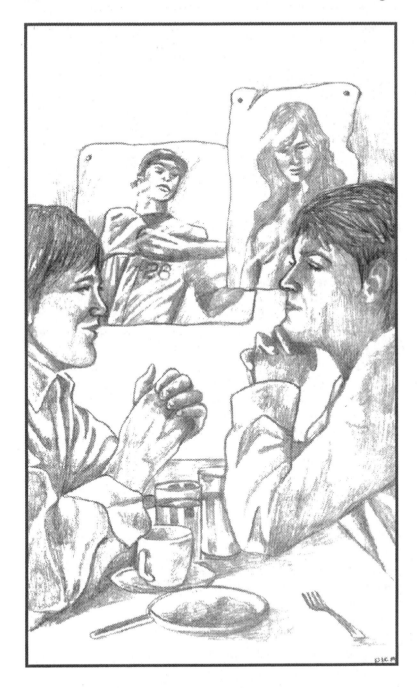

girlfriend. He is interested in the details, but not the reasons; he accepts things as they are and never really wonders about them. It remains a mystery why Meursault becomes involved with Raymond. He doesn't particularly like or dislike Raymond, he just drifts into this encounter in the same way he does everything. He's not particularly interested in a given situation. He doesn't really care when something happens, but when an occasion presents itself, Meursault, perhaps for a lack of anything else to do, simply goes along with it. Although Raymond appears to be a violent, unsavory character, intent on petty revenge, Meursault agrees to write Raymond's letter for him and does so without explaining his reasons.

At the end of Part I, Meursault's strange, indifferent attitude will lead him to the fateful encounter on the beach that will change his life forever.

Study Questions

1. How does Meursault's employer treat him when he returns to work on Monday?

2. Who is Emmanuel?

3. How does Celeste react when he sees Meursault?

4. How long has old Salamano had his dog and why does he abuse him?

5. Who is Raymond Sintes?

6. Why does Raymond want to get revenge on his girlfriend?

7. What does Raymond ask Meursault to do for him?

8. Does Meursault want to be Raymond's friend?

9. What does Raymond say about Meursault's mother?

10. What does Meursault do after he leaves Raymond's room?

Answers

1. Meursault's employer is in a good mood on Monday morning. He offers his sympathy to Meursault and asks how he is feeling.

2. Emmanuel is Meursault's co-worker. At lunchtime they have an adventure running after and leaping onto a truck.

3. Celeste is sympathetic and says she hopes that Meursault isn't "feeling too badly." Meursault tells Celeste he is very hungry.

4. Old Salamano has lived with his dog for eight years. The old man becomes furious when the dog pulls him down the street or gets in his way.

5. Raymond Sintes is Meursault's neighbor. He is a tough young man, reputed to be a pimp.

6. Raymond claims that he is supporting his girlfriend, but that she is cheating on him. He found a lottery ticket and bracelets in her purse, things he never bought for her. He's convinced that some "dirty work" is going on.

7. Raymond wants Meursault to write a letter to the girlfriend for him. He wants to convince the girlfriend to come back to him so that he can beat her up and throw her out again.

8. Meursault accepts Raymond's offer of friendship, but admits to himself that he doesn't care "one way or the other."

9. Raymond says he was sorry to hear that Meursault's mother had died, but it was bound to happen at some point, anyway.

10. Meursault stands alone on the "dank, dark" landing, experiencing the smells and sounds of the hallway.

Suggested Essay Topics

1. Meursault focuses a great deal of attention on the mundane details of his life. Why do you think these details, and his daily routine, are so important to him?

2. How does Meursault feel when he sees old Salamano beating his dog? How does he feel when Raymond tells him he beat up his girlfriend? Discuss Meursault's attitude in relation to these two events.

3. Discuss Meursault's relationship with Raymond. How does he feel about becoming Raymond's "pal," and why would he agree to write such a deceitful letter for him?

Chapter 4

New Characters:

Raymond's Girlfriend: *a young Arab woman*

Policeman: *a police officer who reprimands Raymond*

Summary

Meursault has a busy week at work. Raymond informs Meursault that he has mailed the letter. Meursault and Emmanuel go to see two movies together.

On Saturday, Meursault goes to the beach with Marie. Meursault is attracted to Marie. He likes being with her and looking at her. They enjoy baking in the sun and swimming in the cool sea water. They return to Meursault's apartment where they make love by an open window, savoring the feeling of the cool night air on their sunburned skin.

In the morning, Marie wants to know if Meursault loves her. Meursault seems almost confused by the question. He admits that the question means nothing to him, but he tells her "I supposed I didn't." Marie is disappointed, but doesn't appear to be devastated. She has a pleasant, optimistic personality and she enjoys being with Meursault.

Outside in the hallway they hear old Salamano yelling at his dog. Meursault tells Marie about the old man, and she laughs. Suddenly, they hear a loud commotion coming from Raymond's apartment. A crowd gathers in the hallway; everyone can hear Raymond shouting and beating up his girlfriend. Marie is very disturbed and asks Meursault to call the police, but Meursault refuses and tells her that he doesn't like policemen.

Someone else in the building brings a policeman to Raymond's apartment. The policeman bangs on the door and Raymond, with a smirk on his face, finally opens the door. The policeman smacks

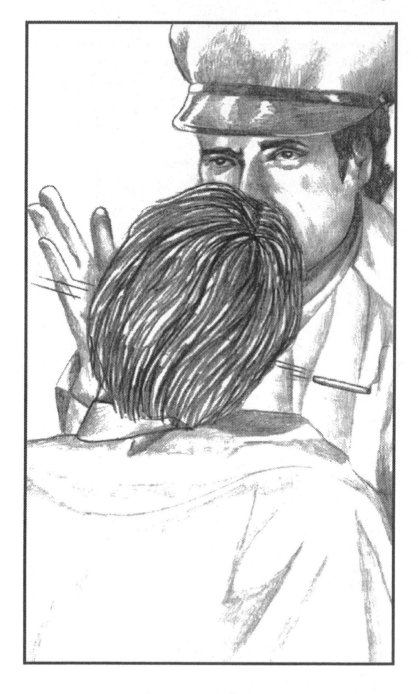

a cigarette out of Raymond's mouth and tells Raymond he must be drunk. Raymond insists he isn't drunk, only nervous because there's a policeman at his door, and shaking from the confrontation. The policeman tells Raymond not to leave his apartment; he'll be summoned to the police station later.

Meursault and Marie return to his apartment. They start to have lunch, but Marie is too upset to eat. She leaves and Meursault takes a nap.

That afternoon, Raymond drops by to get Meursault's opinion about his run-in with the policeman. He is concerned about Meursault's opinion of him, and wonders if Meursault had expected him to fight back. Meursault tells him that he "hadn't expected anything whatsoever." Then Meursault agrees to be Raymond's witness against the girlfriend, even though he doesn't really understand why, or know what he's supposed to say.

Meursault and Raymond go out for a drink. Raymond suggests that they go to a brothel, but Meursault isn't interested. They return to their building and meet old Salamano who is very upset because he has lost his dog. Raymond tells Salamano that lost dogs often return to their masters, but Salamano is convinced that his dog will be taken to the pound and killed. Meursault tells Salamano to check at the pound, but Salamano becomes enraged at the idea of paying money to retrieve the mangy old dog, even though it is obvious that he misses the dog terribly.

Later, Salamano comes to Meursault's room. He's still upset about his dog. Meursault tries to reassure the old man that if he goes to the pound, he'll probably find his dog.

Salamano leaves and returns to his apartment. After a while, Meursault hears him through the wall, weeping alone in his room. Then, "for some reason," Meursault finds himself thinking about his mother. Since he doesn't feel hungry, Meursault goes straight to bed without eating dinner.

Analysis

When Marie asks Meursault if he loves her, he displays his usual detached, indifferent attitude. However, at the same time, he is brutally, and perhaps refreshingly, honest. Given a circumstance where he might be tempted to lie, Meursault can only tell the truth

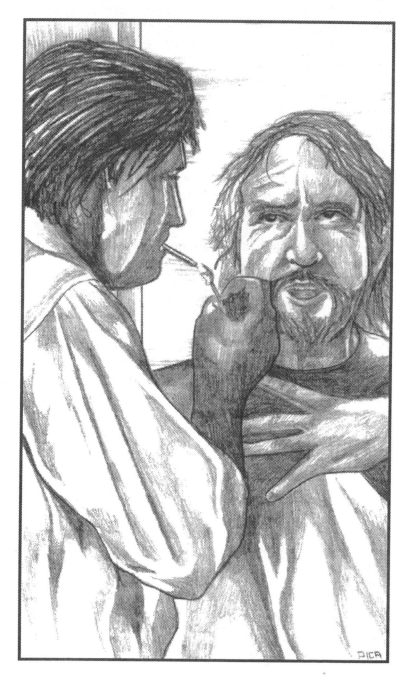

about the way he feels. Most of the time he doesn't have a strong feeling about anything, but he never pretends that he does just to please another person. He is unwilling to commit himself emotionally and it is this intangible quality that may make him interesting and attractive to others.

Meursault's almost emotionless demeanor stands out in sharp contrast to the vivacious Marie, the angry, and then heartbroken Salamano, and the brutal, vindictive Raymond. All three could be drawn to Meursault because of the impassive, seemingly reasonable way he handles most situations. When Raymond vents his anger about his girlfriend, Meursault listens, offering no opinion of Raymond or his actions. Meursault honestly has no opinion, and considering Raymond's cruel behavior toward his girlfriend, Meursault is the perfect ally and sounding board. He doesn't judge anyone. He merely considers whatever it is, words or deeds, that they put before him.

Meursault's kindness towards old Salamano is really just another example of his inability to lie or become emotionally involved in a situation. In this case, he tells Salamano the truth about the dog pound and his words happen to be somewhat reassuring. He understands that the old man is in pain, he hears him crying next door, but he is still unable to make any personal, emotional connection. "For some reason," he says, "I began thinking of Mother." Salamano's grief has obviously triggered some reaction within Meursault. Perhaps it is a feeling that Meursault has suppressed about his mother's death, or it could be Meursault's recognition of the fact that most people mourn in a certain way when they suffer a loss, but in a manner that is completely alien to Meursault.

Study Questions

1. Where do Meursault and Marie go on Saturday?

2. What does Marie do when Meursault tells her about old Salamano and his dog?

3. How does Meursault feel about policemen?

4. How does Raymond greet the policeman who comes to his door?

5. Why is Raymond shaking when he talks to the policeman?

6. How does Meursault feel about being Raymond's witness?

7. Why is old Salamano so upset?

8. How does Raymond treat Salamano?

9. When Salamano visits Meursault, what does Meursault tell him?

10. Why does Meursault think about his mother?

Answers

1. Meursault and Marie go to the beach. Later they return to Meursault's apartment.

2. Marie laughs at Meursault's story.

3. Meursault tells Marie that he doesn't like policemen.

4. Raymond greets the policeman with a "sickly smile" and a cigarette hanging out of his mouth.

5. The policeman accuses Raymond of being drunk, but Raymond says he is shaking because the angry policeman is standing at his door.

6. Meursault says he has no objections, but he doesn't know what Raymond expects him to say.

7. Old Salamano is upset because he lost his dog at the Parade Ground.

8. Raymond tries to reassure Salamano that he'll find his dog again.

9. Meursault tells Salamano that his dog is probably at the pound and won't be killed for at least three days.

10. After he overhears Salamano crying, Meursault, "for some reason," thinks about his mother.

Suggested Essay Topics

1. When Marie asks Meursault if he loves her, he displays an indifferent, almost apathetic attitude towards her. Why would she continue to have a romantic interest in him?

2. Compare Meursault's reaction to Thomas Perez's grief over the mother's death, and his reaction to old Salamano's despair over his lost dog.

3. Considering his indifferent attitude, why would Meursault agree to be Raymond's witness?

4. Since he treats his dog so harshly, why do you think Old Salamano is so upset when the dog runs away?

Chapter 5

New Character:

Robot Woman: *a woman who sits at Meursault's table at Celeste's*

Summary

Raymond telephones Meursault at the office. He invites Meursault and Marie to go to the beach with him on Sunday. He mentions that some Arabs have been following him, and one of them is the brother of his ex-girlfriend. Raymond asks Meursault to watch out for the Arabs and to tell him if he sees them.

The employer calls Meursault into his office to inform him that a branch office is opening in Paris. He asks Meursault if he'd like a job there. The move would be a promotion and the employer thinks he is doing Meursault a favor. Meursault, however, has no interest in moving to Paris; he's content with his life as it is. The employer is puzzled by Meursault's reaction. He admonishes him for lacking ambition.

Meursault returns to his desk, musing over the fact that he used to have "plenty of ambition" when he was a student, but he "soon realized all that was pretty futile."

That night Marie arrives at Meursault's apartment. She asks him to marry her and he agrees, if it will make her happy. However, Meursault doesn't seem to care one way or the other. Marie asks again if Meursault loves her and he tells her no, probably not, and that the question means "nothing, or next to nothing." Then Marie asks if he'd marry any girl who asked him and he replies, "Naturally." Marie questions her own love for Meursault and adds that she thinks he's a "queer fellow." Meursault offers no opinion on any of this.

Meursault tells Marie about his employer's offer to transfer him to Paris. Marie is interested in living in Paris, but Meursault says that Paris is a dark, dirty city. Then Marie leaves Meursault to dine alone, telling him she has other plans for the evening. Meursault doesn't bother to ask Marie what her plans are until she prompts him to do so.

Meursault has dinner by himself at Celeste's. While he is sitting at his usual table, an "odd-looking little woman" asks Meursault if she could sit with him. Meursault has no objections so the woman sits and orders her meal. She ignores Meursault and pores over the menu, adds up the bill in advance, and moves in an abrupt, mechanical way. Meursault spends his time studying her, taking in every detail. When she leaves the restaurant, Meursault follows her for a few blocks, thinking of her as "the little robot."

Meursault returns to his apartment and meets Salamano who tells him that his dog never returned. Meursault is not particularly interested in Salamano's problems but he listens to the old man because he has nothing else to do. Salamano tells Meursault that when he was a young man he wanted to be in the theater, but ended up taking a job with the railroad instead. He had an unhappy marriage, but was lonely when his wife died, so he got a puppy to keep him company. Meursault tells him that the dog always looked well bred. Salamano is pleased and says that Meursault's mother had always been fond of the dog.

On his way out of Meursault's apartment, Salamano mentions that some of Meursault's neighbors said "nasty things" about him when he put his mother in the nursing home. Meursault is surprised to hear this; he explains to Salamano that it was the best thing for her. Salamano agrees, telling Meursault that he knows Meursault was always devoted to his mother.

Analysis

When Meursault turns down the job in Paris, his employer accuses him of lacking ambition. Meursault apparently agrees with this, but he doesn't admit to being lazy. His lack of ambition stems from his realization that the ambition he had as a youth was "pretty futile." Meursault refuses to conform to the standards and conduct followed by the majority. Not only is he content with the life he is leading, but he sees no value in trying to improve himself or "move up the ladder" in the conventional sense. He has no interest in or reason to accept the "change of life" his employer suggests.

For similar reasons, Meursault does agree to marry Marie, but he admits he doesn't care if they wed or not. He's glad to do so if it will make Marie happy. He enjoys being with her, enjoys it when she laughs, however, he doesn't love her. Marie has become part of Meursault's routine and marrying her would probably not alter it in any significant way. Although Marie is put off by Meursault's blunt admissions, she still wants to be with him, giving in to an attraction that she does not fully understand. She tells Meursault that he's a "queer fellow" and that's why she loves him, but she also fears that this same odd quality of Meursault's may one day make her "hate" him.

Meursault is intrigued by the robot woman and even follows her down the street. Her machine-like qualities set her apart from normal society, too. She moves along in her own world, seemingly oblivious to what others may think about her. Meursault exhibits similar traits as he interacts with others and goes about his daily routine.

Meursault's idiosyncratic manner is not as obvious as the robot woman's. He nevertheless sets himself apart from the norm, keeping himself removed from what is usually accepted as ordinary conduct. This is not so much by a rigid appearance, but by the actions he takes, his opinions or lack of them, and his indifferent, detached attitude towards everyone and everything. When Salamano tells him that neighbors have criticized him for putting his mother in a nursing home, Meursault is very surprised. His lack of emotion regarding his mother is something he accepts as normal and perfectly logical and he can't understand why others might be repelled by how he acts and thinks. Later in the story, society will take a harsh view of Meursault's unusual opinions and behavior.

Study Questions

1. Where does Raymond want to go on Sunday with Meursault and Marie?

2. What does Meursault's employer suggest during their meeting?

3. How does Meursault feel about Paris?

4. What does Marie ask Meursault?

5. Does Meursault want to marry Marie?

6. With whom does Meursault eat at Celeste's?

7. What does Meursault notice about the "robot" woman?

8. What was Salamano's occupation?

9. According to Salamano, what do Meursault's neighbors say about him?

10. Why did Meursault put his mother in the nursing home?

Answers

1. He wants to go to a friend's seaside bungalow just outside Algiers.

2. The employer suggests that Meursault take a job in the new branch office in Paris.

3. Meursault has no interest in living in Paris. He thinks it is a dingy town with masses of pigeons and dark courtyards.

4. Marie asks Meursault if he loves her and if he will marry her.

5. Meursault doesn't care. He says he doesn't "mind" and agrees to marry Marie if it will make her happy.

6. The "little robot" woman eats at Meursault's table in Celeste's.

7. Meursault watches the robot woman study the menu, add up the bill, and march off down the street in a stiff, mechanical fashion.

8. Salamano worked for the railroad.

9. Meursault's neighbors say "nasty things" about Meursault because he put his mother in the nursing home.

10. Meursault explains that he couldn't afford to keep his mother at home. In addition, they never spoke to each other and she was "moping with no one to talk to."

Suggested Essay Topics

1. When the employer offers Meursault a new job, he suggests that a "change of life" might be good for him. Why would Meursault turn down the job in Paris?

2. Discuss Meursault's feelings for Marie. He says he doesn't love her, yet he wants to make her happy. Why would Meursault agree to marry Marie?

3. Discuss Meursault's fascination with the "little robot" woman and her odd, mechanical actions.

Chapter 6

New Characters:

The Arab: *Raymond's girlfriend's brother*

Second Arab: *The Arab's companion*

Masson: *Raymond's friend who owns a small bungalow on the beach*

Mme. Masson: *Masson's wife*

Summary

When Meursault wakes up on Sunday he doesn't feel well, but he's agreed to go out with Marie and Raymond. Marie tries to cheer Meursault up and jokes that he looks like a "mourner at a funeral." Meursault admits to feeling "limp."

Standing outside on the street, the sun glares into Meursault's eyes. Marie is in good spirits, however, and soon Meursault is feeling better. Raymond arrives wearing a straw hat, looking very dapper, but Meursault is put off by his getup. Meursault recalls going to the police station the night before to testify for Raymond. The

police did not check Meursault's statement and they let Raymond off with just a warning.

On the way to the bus stop they notice a group of Arab men staring at them. Raymond says that one of them is his girlfriend's brother. Marie nervously urges them on to the bus stop.

They arrive at the beach and Marie is in good spirits again. She happily swings her bag as they walk along by the water. They arrive at Raymond's friend Masson's beach house. Raymond introduces Masson and his wife to Meursault and Marie. Marie and Mme. Masson laugh and talk together, and Meursault indicates that he is seriously considering marrying Marie.

Meursault and Marie go swimming together and have an enjoyable time. They return to Masson's bungalow, drink wine, and eat a big lunch. Meursault starts to feel slightly drunk. He talks about possibly spending the month of August on the beach with Masson and Raymond. Everyone is enjoying themselves and they realize they have all lost track of time when Marie notices that it is only 11:30 in the morning.

Meursault, Raymond, and Masson walk back down to the beach. Meursault is bothered by the sun glaring off the water. He feels groggy and a little confused.

As they walk along the beach, two Arab men approach them. Raymond realizes that one of the men is his girlfriend's brother. Raymond and his girlfriend's brother fight while Masson goes for the other Arab. During the fight, the Arab pulls a knife and cuts Raymond on the arm and mouth. Both Arabs run off down the beach.

Masson takes the bleeding Raymond to a doctor to have his wounds treated. Meursault returns to the bungalow where Marie and Mme. Masson want to know what happened on the beach. But Meursault stands off by himself, staring out at the sea, refusing to discuss the incident.

Raymond returns from the doctor and goes for a walk on the beach. Meursault follows him and once again they encounter the two Arabs. Raymond has brought a gun with him and he asks Meursault if he should shoot one of the Arabs. Meursault tells him not to shoot unless the Arab pulls a knife. Then Meursault asks Raymond to give him the gun. He tells himself that it doesn't

matter if the gun is fired or not because "it would come to absolutely the same thing."

The four men stare at each other for a moment and then the two Arabs walk away.

Meursault and Raymond return to the bungalow. Raymond goes inside, but Meursault feels too tired to bother walking up the steps. He can't decide if he should go into the bungalow or not, but then it occurs to him that no matter what he decides, it doesn't really matter. So Meursault returns to the beach by himself, bothered even more now by the blinding sunlight. He walks on, accusing the sun of making him feel tense and confused, searching for a cool stream he and Raymond had found earlier.

Meursault reaches the stream and discovers the Arab sitting there, leaning against a rock. Meursault realizes that he could walk away, but he steps forward instead and the Arab pulls out his knife. Sun glints off the knife blade and a blinding shaft of light shoots into Meursault's face. Meursault feels the light stabbing into his forehead. "Then everything began to reel before my eyes." Meursault feels his finger squeezing the trigger of the gun in his pocket. He shoots the Arab once, then deliberately fires four more bullets into his body. Meursault tells us, "I knew I'd shattered the balance of the day and the spacious calm of this beach on which I had been happy."

Analysis

On Sunday, Meursault has difficulty waking up and Marie has to shake him to get him out of bed. He doesn't feel well, he has a headache, and he complains that his first cigarette tastes "bitter." Meursault may not want to get out of bed at all. The Sunday before he chose to stay in his apartment all day, by himself, staring out the window. But now he has made a commitment to two other people. He has subtly changed his routine by allowing himself to get involved with others. Meursault expects some misfortune to befall him if he deviates from his usual habits, and the disastrous events that occur on the beach certainly justify his apprehensions.

Meursault has allowed change to enter his life. He has new friends, a lover whom he is considering marrying, and he is even

thinking about taking a month off to vacation on the beach. While he considers these possibilities, the action he takes on the beach belies his best intentions. He purposely takes Raymond's gun, having earlier had too much to drink, and goes off for a walk by himself. Although he seems genuinely surprised when he meets the Arab, could it be that somewhere in his subconscious Meursault was aware of the possibility of another encounter? Why would Meursault deliberately sabotage his own life?

Just as he answers people's questions with his blunt, yet indifferent honesty, Meursault finds himself reacting instinctively during his confrontation with the Arab. Earlier he stated that it made no difference if Raymond had pulled the trigger of his revolver. He offers a similar opinion about simply going up the stairs to the bungalow. "To stay or to make a move—it came to much the same." With the oppressive sun and heat clouding his mind, Meursault chooses not to go inside, but to walk back to the beach. Had he taken the other path and gone into the bungalow, the results of his action would have been very different. But for Meursault, apparently, it makes no difference. To him, the significance of either action and its result may be the same.

Study Questions

1. How does Meursault feel when he wakes up on Sunday morning?

2. Where does Meursault first see the Arabs?

3. What does Meursault think about Raymond's outfit?

4. Who is Masson?

5. How does Meursault feel after he eats lunch?

6. Where do Meursault, Raymond, and Masson go after lunch?

7. What happens when Raymond fights with the Arab?

8. What does Raymond do when he meets the Arab again?

9. How does the sun affect Meursault when he's walking alone on the beach?

10. What happens when Meursault confronts the Arab?

Answers

1. Meursault wakes up with a headache, feeling "under the weather."

2. He sees them standing around in front of the tobacconist's shop.

3. Meursault is "put off by his getup."

4. Masson is Raymond's friend. He owns the bungalow on the beach.

5. Meursault complains of feeling "slightly muzzy."

6. They go for a walk on the beach and they encounter the two Arabs.

7. The Arab pulls a knife and cuts Raymond on the face and arm.

8. The second time Raymond meets the Arab, he considers shooting him, but Meursault talks him out of it.

9. Meursault experiences a "dark befuddlement" when the intense sunlight "blasts" into his face.

10. With the sun "stabbing" into his face, Meursault shoots the Arab five times and kills him.

Suggested Essay Topics

1. Discuss Meursault's reaction to the sunlight. How does it affect his moods and actions?

2. Why does Meursault talk Raymond out of shooting the Arab?

3. When Meursault shoots the Arab he tells us: "I knew I'd shattered the balance of the day..." What does he mean by this?

4. Why do you think Meursault is so reluctant to tell Marie and Madam Masson about the confrontation with the Arabs?

SECTION THREE

Part Two

Chapter 1

New Characters:

Examining Magistrate: *a court representative who interrogates Meursault*

The Lawyer: *Meursault's young, court-appointed defense attorney*

Summary

Following the murder of the Arab, Meursault has been arrested. He describes how he was questioned several times, first by the police and then by the examining magistrate.

Alone in his cell, Meursault recalls meeting the magistrate who asks him if he has a lawyer. Meursault replies no, he didn't think it was necessary and hadn't really thought about it. He assumed that his case would be "very simple." However, the magistrate tells him that they must abide by the law and the Court will appoint an attorney for him. Meursault thinks that this is an "excellent arrangement."

During the interview, Meursault pays great attention to the physical details of the interrogation room, commenting on the furnishings and the way the light shines from a desk lamp. He finds that the examining magistrate is an intelligent and pleasant man, although he notices that he has a "rather ugly twist" to his mouth.

The next day, the court appointed attorney visits Meursault in his cell. He tells Meursault that the police have been checking into his private life and have been investigating his behavior following

the death of his mother. The police were informed that Meursault showed "great callousness" at the time of the funeral. The lawyer asks him if he felt grief when his mother died. Meursault replies that in recent years he'd lost touch with his feelings. He tells the lawyer that most people, at one time or another, have wished for the death of a loved one. However, he adds, he wishes his mother hadn't died.

The lawyer instructs Meursault not to repeat such a statement in court. Meursault tells him that he finds it difficult to predict how he might act on any given occasion. His behavior is greatly affected by his mood and by the way he feels physically. Finally, Meursault agrees to the lawyer's request, but just to "satisfy him," he tells us.

The lawyer informs Meursault that witnesses from the nursing home will be called to testify against him. Meursault doesn't understand what bearing this would have on his case. The lawyer tells him that, obviously, Meursault doesn't understand the legal system. The lawyer leaves, annoyed at Meursault and dissatisfied with his answers. Meursault senses the lawyer's displeasure and tells us that he wanted to explain to the lawyer that he was "quite an ordinary person," but he decided not to "out of laziness as much as anything else."

Meursault has another interview with the examining magistrate. The room is hot and bright. The magistrate tells Meursault that his lawyer is unable to attend this session, but Meursault says it doesn't matter, he can answer for himself.

The magistrate mentions that he is interested in Meursault personally. Meursault describes his day on the beach and the shooting of the Arab. The magistrate says he will try to help Meursault, then he asks him if he loved his mother. Meursault replies, "Yes, like everybody else." The magistrate then asks Meursault why he fired five consecutive shots at the Arab. Meursault tells him that the shots were not consecutive. He fired once, then four more times. The magistrate demands to know why Meursault fired the other four shots, but Meursault cannot answer him. He can only remember the feeling of the sun at the beach, burning on his face.

The magistrate becomes very angry and holds up a silver crucifix. He talks about the need to repent, and how even the worst

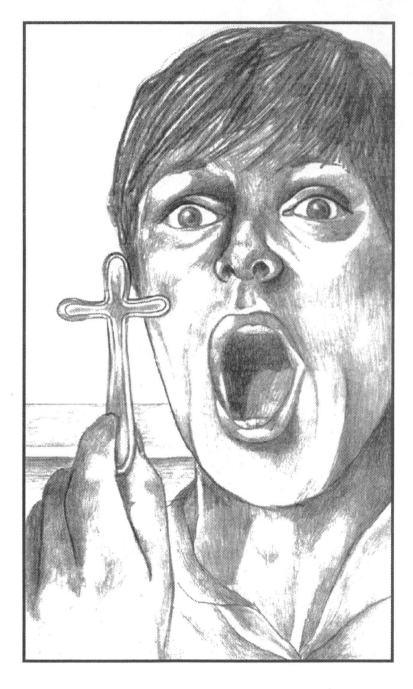

of sinners could obtain forgiveness if they believed in God. Meursault sits there feeling very uncomfortable because of the heat in the room and the flies buzzing around his face. He has difficulty getting a word in as the magistrate goes on and on. Finally, the magistrate asks Meursault if he believes in God and Meursault says, "No." However, the magistrate says that this is "unthinkable." He keeps pressing the issue until Meursault finally agrees with him just to end the conversation. But in the end, when the magistrate asks him again if he believes in God, Meursault shakes his head no.

The magistrate says he has never met a "soul so case–hardened" as Meursault. Most criminals weep at the sight of the crucifix, but not him. Finally the magistrate asks Meursault if he regrets his crime and Meursault tells him he feels not so much regret, but "a kind of vexation." The magistrate doesn't understand what he means and he ends the interview.

The case progresses and the investigation goes on for 11 more months. During this time, Meursault is interviewed on many more occasions by his lawyer and the magistrate. He notes that during the sessions they all get along very well, treating each other in a friendly manner. "I had the absurd impression," Meursault says, "of being one of the family." Meursault feels very comfortable chatting with the two men and tells us that sometimes, at the end of a session, the magistrate would walk him to the door, pat his shoulder in a friendly way and say, "Well, Mr. Anti-Christ, that's all for the present!"

Analysis

The murder of the Arab dramatically alters Meursault's day-to-day existence. No longer free to work at his job, eat at Celeste's, or go out with Marie, he spends his days in a small jail cell, awaiting his trial. However, Meursault seems to adapt rather quickly to his new situation. By the end of Chapter One, 11 months have passed and he has settled into the new routine of prison life and visiting with the magistrate and his court-appointed lawyer. Although he finds himself in the most dire of circumstances, Meursault responds to it all in his usual indifferent, slightly bemused manner. While he has a passing interest in the legal system, he does not relate it to his own situation. Meursault is happy to cooperate with the authorities and his own lawyer, but he takes no direct action to help himself.

Meursault is genuinely surprised by the reaction of others to the way he acts and the statements he makes. The lawyer is shocked when Meursault does not express any profound feeling of grief over his mother's death, and he is astounded by Meursault's naiveté concerning the legal system. The lawyer is well aware that society will take a dim view of Meursault's behavior at his mother's funeral and his lack of obvious grief over her death. He understands that this could be used against Meursault when he goes to trial for killing the Arab. However Meursault doesn't comprehend any of this. He considers himself "like everybody else; quite an ordinary person." Consequently, with each answer he gives, Meursault digs a deeper hole for himself. But Meursault has nothing to hide. He thinks his reactions are normal, so why should society condemn him for them?

Meursault begins to feel more alienated when the magistrate confronts him with the crucifix. Once again Meursault has no reason to lie. When asked if he believes in God, Meursault says no, and it is this answer that perhaps seals his fate. The magistrate cannot bear having his own belief questioned, or even worse, dismissed. He believes his own life would have no meaning if there were no God. Therefore, it becomes intolerable for him when Meursault can't even pretend that he believes in God.

The magistrate's only option is to classify Meursault in his mind as a hardened criminal, the worst he's ever seen, incapable of remorse or salvation. Meursault doesn't believe in God, therefore he is incapable of distinguishing between right and wrong; there is no immortal consequence to deter him from immoral action. Once the magistrate has come to this conclusion, he doesn't even try to reach Meursault with his own religious convictions. He's content to chat with him during their subsequent meetings, and even joke with Meursault about his disbelief in God. The magistrate's faith, and very reason for being, remains secure once he has decided that Meursault is beyond redemption; and as society's legal representative, the magistrate has the power to eliminate Meursault and everything he represents.

While Meursault is secure in his own opinions about God and an afterlife, his lack of faith offers him no hope for eternal salvation. He cannot enjoy the kind of conventional comfort a belief in God might provide a person in Meursault's circumstance.

Study Questions

1. What does Meursault think about the magistrate when he first meets him?

2. What does Meursault's lawyer look like?

3. What charge against Meursault, besides murder, is the lawyer concerned about?

4. Is the lawyer optimistic about Meursault's case?

5. How did Meursault feel about his mother?

6. How does the lawyer react to Meursault during their first meeting?

7. What does the typist do during Meursault's meeting with the magistrate?

8. How does Meursault react to the magistrate when the magistrate starts talking about God?

9. How does Meursault feel sitting in the magistrate's office?

10. Does Meursault accept the fact that he is a criminal?

Answers

1. Meursault finds him to be "highly intelligent and, on the whole, likable enough."

2. The lawyer is a "small, plump, youngish man with sleek, black hair."

3. He is concerned about the charge of "callousness."

4. When the lawyer first meets with Meursault, he tells him that he has a good chance of getting off, if Meursault follows his advice.

5. Meursault tells the lawyer that he had been "quite fond of Mother."

6. He is repulsed by Meursault and annoyed at his answers.

7. The clerk types an answer he assumes Meursault will give to the magistrate's question about Meursault's mother, but then has to cross it out when Meursault responds differently than expected.

8. Meursault says, "He rather alarmed me."

9. He feels hot, uncomfortable, and bothered by annoying flies.

10. Meursault tells us: "Somehow it was an idea to which I never could get reconciled."

Suggested Essay Topics

1. Meursault doesn't explain why he assumes his case will be "very simple." Discuss the reasons why Meursault might feel this way.

2. Why is the magistrate so upset when he talks to Meursault about God?

3. Why is the lawyer worried about Meursault's behavior at his mother's funeral?

Chapter 2

New Character:

Chief Jailer: *a prison guard*

Summary

Meursault describes his life in prison. He explains that at first he felt reluctant to talk about this period of his life. Marie is not allowed in to see him, because she is not a relative. Meursault begins to understand that from now on, the prison will be his home.

When Meursault is first arrested he is put in a large cell with several other men, mostly Arabs. The men ask what he did to get arrested and Meursault tells them he killed an Arab. The men keep silent for a while, but soon they become friendlier and help him adjust to prison life. After a few days Meursault is moved to a small cell by himself. The cell has a tiny window and Meursault is able to look out and see the sunlight glancing off the water.

Marie visits Meursault in the noisy visiting room. Meursault feels "squeamish" and uncomfortable. The sun, streaming through the windows, creates a harsh glare. Meursault and Marie are forced to exchange greetings, shouting over the noise, surrounded by many other prisoners and their families. Meursault has a great desire to reach out and touch Marie, but they are separated by a divider. Marie tells Meursault everything will be all right. Soon they'll get married and be able to go swimming again.

Marie writes to Meursault and tells him she won't be allowed to visit him anymore. Meursault longs to be out of prison, and to go swimming again, but he realizes that his "habit of thinking like a free man" will only cause him grief. So he begins to think like a prisoner, waiting for his exercise time and visits from his lawyer. Gradually Meursault adjusts and begins to manage, he tells us, "quite well."

Meursault spends his time thinking about his past. He desires cigarettes and women. He becomes friendly with the chief jailer, who informs him that most prisoners complain about not being able to be with a woman. Meursault reasons that this condition is particularly unfair, but the jailer tells him that prisoners are punished precisely because they are being deprived of their liberty. Meursault understands what he means.

Meursault passes the time by recalling the various furnishings in his apartment, listing each object in every room. He decides that a man could live a hundred years in prison providing he had spent a least one day of freedom out in the world. He would have more than enough memories to fill the hours. Meursault also kills time by sleeping. Gradually he sleeps more and more, until eventually he is sleeping "sixteen or eighteen hours" each day.

One day while poking around under his straw mattress, Meursault discovers an old newspaper clipping that describes a murder that occurred in Czechoslovakia. A rich man returned from overseas to visit the small village where he grew up. He checked into a hotel run by his mother and sister, but they didn't recognize him. He registered under a false name in order to surprise them later. But that night the mother and sister killed him for his money. When the man's wife arrived the next day, she revealed his true

identity. Upon learning the news, the man's mother hung herself and his sister threw herself into a well.

Meursault decides the man in the article was "asking for trouble" by playing tricks, but he is intrigued by the story and he reads it over and over again.

As the months slip by, Meursault loses track of time. One day the jailer informs him that he's been in prison for six months, but to Meursault it seems like it's been one long day. He studies his own face in a tin dish and notices that he has a "mournful, tense expression." Meursault has a hard time at the end of each day, watching the sun set from his little window. He realizes that he's been talking to himself when he finally recognizes the sound of his own voice.

Analysis

When Marie tells Meursault she won't be allowed to visit him again, Meursault begins to understand what his loss of freedom really means, and he gains a new appreciation of the sensual and intellectual pleasures that he enjoyed in the outside world. However, in his usual fashion, he is able to adapt to his new situation. He finds ways to pass the time and occupy his mind; he even makes a new friend in the chief jailer. However, he can't help but long for a cigarette and the company of a woman. He peers out through his tiny window, catching a pleasant glimpse of the sea and sky, but dreading the end of the day. When the sun sets, Meursault must prepare himself for another long night and the reality of his harsh environment becomes all too apparent.

After Meursault discovers the newspaper clipping about the murder in Czechoslovakia, he spends hours rereading it and thinking about it. Unlike Meursault's crime, this murder has been motivated by greed and was planned in advance by the victim's mother and sister. The motivation for murder is far less obvious in Meursault's case, however, and although the prosecutor will argue differently, the crime appears to have been a spontaneous act. But Meursault, himself, never gives a clear reason for what he did, other than to try to explain about the sun. The contrast between the two murders is obvious, yet the result—a murderer and a victim—remains the same.

The sunlight again plays an important part in affecting Meursault's moods and comfort in prison despite the fact that he is deprived of his freedom and direct contact with the natural environment. From his jail cell, Meursault enjoys watching the sunlight dance off the waves in the sea, but in the Visitors' Room, this same light takes on an oppressive quality, "surging" against the windows, flooding into the room, and distorting people's faces. Just as the sunlight on the beach moved Meursault to behave in a certain manner—adding to his enjoyment of a moment, or leading him to kill the Arab—the light he observes in the prison can also affect him in a number of ways.

The sun is an impartial, yet powerful force, one that strongly influences Meursault. It is an influence that he acknowledges, but finds difficult to explain. When his trial begins, Meursault will attempt to explain the effect the sun had on him at the beach. He will be hard pressed to come up with any kind of a rational explanation, one at least that society will be willing to accept, for killing the Arab.

Study Questions

1. What does Meursault hope for when he's first put in prison?

2. How does the Arab prisoner help out Meursault?

3. What does Meursault feel the first night he spends in jail?

4. How far apart are the prisoners kept from their visitors?

5. What does Meursault long for when he sees Marie?

6. What does Marie do when Meursault is led back out of the Visitors' Room?

7. Why does the jailer think Meursault is different?

8. Besides women, what else are the prisoners deprived of?

9. As Meursault loses track of time, what are the two words that still have meaning for him?

10. What does Meursault use for a mirror?

Answers

1. Meursault has a "vague hope" that something good will happen, some "agreeable surprise."
2. He shows him how to make a pillow with his sleeping mat.
3. Meursault feels bugs crawling on his face.
4. They are separated by a "gap of some thirty feet."
5. He wants to reach out and squeeze her shoulders.
6. She throws him a kiss.
7. The jailer tells Meursault he's different because he can think and "use his brains."
8. Smoking is also forbidden in the prison.
9. The words "yesterday" and "tomorrow" still have meaning.
10. He uses a polished "tin pannikin."

Suggested Essay Topics

1. Discuss how Meursault's behavior and way of thinking change as he spends time in prison.
2. Why would Meursault tell the Arab prisoners about his crime? Why wouldn't he consider inventing a story to protect himself?
3. Discuss why Meursault becomes so fascinated with the Czechoslovakian murder story.
4. Considering the atmosphere in the visiting room, why do you think Marie is so cheerful and optimistic when she visits Meursault?

Chapter 3

New Characters:

Court Policeman: *the officer guarding Meursault in court*

Journalist: *a reporter covering Meursault's trial*

The Public Prosecutor: *the attorney who aggressively seeks Meursault's conviction*

The Judge: *the chief justice who presides over the trial*

Summary

Meursault's trial begins. His lawyer tells him the case won't take longer than two or three days because another, more important trial is scheduled to begin when Meursault's concludes. The other trial is a case of parricide—a son has been arrested for killing his father—and there has been much publicity surrounding it.

As Meursault awaits the start of his trial, he sits in a small room outside the court. He listens, merely as an observer, to various sounds inside the courtroom: the scraping of chairs, and all the shouts and "hubbub." Meursault tells one of the policemen guarding him that he's interested in watching a trial because he's never seen one before.

Inside the courtroom the heat is intense. Meursault notices the sunlight coming through the blinds on the windows. Meursault stares at the jury members and they regard him. He looks out at the big crowd in the courtroom and comments on its size. The policeman tells him that the press has been reporting on his case and has drummed up a lot of public interest.

A journalist approaches Meursault and tells him that the newspaper he works for wrote about Meursault's case for a number of months when things were slow and there wasn't much else to report. However, most of the people in court are here for the parricide trial. Meursault begins to feel out of place, as if he were crashing a party to which he hadn't been invited.

The public prosecutor, Meursault's lawyer, and the three judges arrive. Meursault notices a young journalist staring at him and Meursault gets the peculiar feeling that he is being studied by himself.

The list of witnesses is read out, and Meursault is surprised to see all the people he knows, including Marie, Raymond, Masson, Salamano, Thomas Perez, the doorkeeper, and Celeste. Then Meursault sees the odd robot woman sitting in the courtroom.

The judge begins to question Meursault. He asks him questions about his identity, questions Meursault has answered many times before. Meursault reasons that they keep asking him these questions so they won't make a mistake and try the wrong man. Then the judge asks Meursault why he sent his mother to the nursing home. Meursault tells the court that he and his mother never "expected much from one another," so they both had gotten used to the situation.

The prosecutor stands and asks Meursault if, when he returned to the stream, he intended to kill the Arab. Meursault says no, he found himself back at the stream purely as a matter of chance. The prosecutor ends his questioning, looking at Meursault with contempt.

Next, the judge questions the warden of the nursing home. The warden tells the court that Meursault's mother used to complain about her son, but that was not unusual, as most of the residents griped about their families. But he adds, after further questioning, that Meursault didn't seem interested in viewing his mother's body and that he hadn't "shed a single tear."

The prosecutor concludes his questioning with a look of triumph on his face and Meursault experiences an unusual rush of emotion. He suddenly feels like crying, convinced that everyone connected to the case hates him.

Next, the doorkeeper takes the witness stand and describes how Meursault drank coffee, smoked, and dozed during the vigil. He says that Meursault didn't want to see his mother's body. Meursault's lawyer points out that it was the doorkeeper who offered Meursault the coffee, but the prosecutor maintains that Meursault should have refused the coffee out of respect for his mother.

Thomas Perez is the next witness. He describes his own feelings of grief during the funeral and says he didn't pay much attention to Meursault. However, Perez admits, he doesn't believe Meursault ever cried.

Celeste testifies on Meursault's behalf and tells the court that Meursault is a fairly quiet person. Celeste believes that the murder was "just an accident." The judge cuts him off before he can fully explain what he means. Celeste steps down and Meursault feels grateful to him for his efforts.

Marie takes the stand after Celeste. The prosecutor asks her when she began her affair with Meursault. Marie confesses it was the day after his mother's funeral and admits that they went to see a comic film that night. The prosecutor makes much of this statement and Marie bursts into tears. She tries to tell the court that her statements were misunderstood, that she had been bullied by the prosecutor, and that Meursault had done nothing wrong. A court officer leads her out of the courtroom.

Masson, the next witness, testifies that Meursault is "a respectable young fellow" and a "decent chap." He is followed by old Salamano who tells the court that Meursault was very kind to him and his dog. However, no one seems to care about what either man has said.

Raymond Sintes is the final witness. He explains that he was the one who had a problem with the Arab, not Meursault. Meursault, he says, just happened to be there. The prosecutor asks why Meursault wrote the letter to Raymond's girlfriend. Raymond replies that it was "due to mere chance." The prosecutor scoffs at this explanation. He reveals that Raymond beat up his girlfriend and Meursault did nothing to stop him. He goes on to describe Raymond as a man who lives off "the immoral earnings of women." Raymond says that he and Meursault are good friends. The prosecutor uses this opportunity to say that Meursault was obviously involved with Raymond in some type of criminal vendetta, and that this is the reason he killed the Arab. He calls Meursault "an inhuman monster, wholly without a moral sense."

Meursault's lawyer tries to defend him, pointing out the irrelevance of all the testimony about Meursault's mother. But the prosecutor argues that someone who doesn't cry at his own mother's funeral must be a criminal at heart.

Back in his cell, dreading the long night ahead of him, Meursault recalls when he was free and would sit outside, experiencing the sights and sounds of a warm summer evening. Meursault remembers it as a time when he felt "so well content with life."

Analysis

In dealing with the prosecutor, Meursault is confronted by an element of society that causes him considerable confusion. From the outset of the trial it appears that the prosecutor is not so much interested in eliciting the truth as much as he is in winning the case. Of course, the fact remains that Meursault did kill the Arab, shooting him not once, but five times. The court wants to hear some kind of a reasonable explanation from Meursault, but as usual, he is completely at odds with society. Meursault has great difficulty explaining himself, and the reason he does give—the glaring sun—sounds ridiculous and satisfies no one. Meursault does not consciously choose to antagonize the court; he tries his best to be honest. But the truth for Meursault contains an explanation that leaves the court, and society, mystified. The prosecutor seizes the opportunity to condemn Meursault as an immoral, cold-blooded killer.

The first questions Meursault must answer concern his mother and the reasons he put her in the nursing home. Questions that follow have to do with Meursault's feelings, or lack of feelings, for his mother and his behavior at her funeral. Witnesses are called to corroborate the prosecutor's assertion that Meursault is a heartless criminal by describing his actions following his mother's death. Later his relationship with Marie is dissected and held up to similar scrutiny. But what does any of this have to do with Meursault's crime? Meursault is perplexed and he finds it impossible to argue with any of the evidence presented. Is he being tried for a murder or for his unconventional behavior? And why does his own lawyer seem so eager to defend him against charges that have nothing to do with the case?

When Meursault responds to the prosecutor's questions, it doesn't occur to him to lie, or even to shade the truth in a way that might present his situation in a more favorable light. He simply tells the truth about his feelings or his perception of a certain circumstance. Although he has an opportunity to tell the court that he loved his mother and grieved after her death, as we have seen, this is not what happened. Meursault can't lie about this, just as he can't lie about why he shot the Arab. Besides finding most of the questions irrelevant and incomprehensible, he can't imagine making up some story to save himself.

In the past, Meursault regarded many social conventions with an indifferent attitude, and his behavior set him apart from the majority of his community. Now he must answer to that community, but when he refuses to tell society what it wants to hear, society condemns him. He is cut off from the things he loves most, the sensual, daily pleasures of the natural world that made his life enjoyable. However, once the trial adjourns for the day and he is alone in his cell, Meursault begins to gain an even greater appreciation for the things in the past that made his life worthwhile. He is also painfully aware that he may never again have the opportunity to enjoy these things, and the deprivation that society has imposed on him may last forever.

Study Questions

1. During what month does Meursault's trial begin?

2. What does the special news correspondent from Paris look like?

3. How many judges preside over Meursault's trial?

4. What is the first thing the judge questions Meursault about?

5. What does the judge ask Meursault about his mother?

6. Following Meursault, who is the first witness called?

7. What does the doorkeeper say about Meursault?

8. Who does the defense call as its first witness?

9. What does Marie do at the conclusion of her testimony?

10. Who is the last witness?

Answers

1. The trial begins in June.
2. He is a small, plump man who reminds Meursault of an "overfed weasel."
3. There are three. Two are in black robes and one is in scarlet.
4. Meursault must answer questions about his identity.
5. The judge wants to know why Meursault sent her to the home.
6. The warden of the nursing home is the first witness.
7. The doorkeeper testifies that during the vigil over his mother's body, Meursault slept, smoked cigarettes, and drank coffee.
8. Celeste is the defense's first witness.
9. She bursts into tears.
10. Raymond is the last witness.

Suggested Essay Topics

1. Discuss how Meursault's feelings and attitude change about his trial as he observes the courtroom proceedings.
2. Why would the prosecutor ask Marie questions about her relationship with Meursault? Does the prosecutor really consider this an important aspect of the case? Explain your answer.
3. Meursault has difficulty trying to explain why he killed the Arab. What do you think his motivation could have been?
4. Although Meursault has adapted to the daily routine of the prison, he begins to realize that he misses many of the pleasures he took for granted when he was a free man. Has Meursault changed since he killed the Arab? How is he different, or the same?

Chapter 4

Summary

The trial continues. For a while, Meursault is interested in listening to other people talk about him. For once, he is tempted to speak in his own defense, but his lawyer advises him not to say anything. Gradually, he begins to lose interest in what the judges and lawyers are saying about him.

When the prosecutor delivers his closing argument, Meursault grows weary of listening to him. The only thing that interests him are the man's elaborate gestures and occasional loud tirades. The prosecutor describes Meursault's background, his relationships with Marie and Raymond, and calls Meursault an intelligent man. He says Meursault knew what he was doing and never showed remorse for his crime. Meursault wishes he could tell the prosecutor that in all his life, he has never been able to feel regret for anything. He has always lived for the present moment, or the immediate future.

The prosecutor then describes Meursault as an immoral man whose soul is "blank." While Meursault can't be blamed for his lack of conscience, he is still a danger to society. He relates Meursault's case to the upcoming parricide trial; he says that Meursault is "morally guilty" of his own mother's death. There is no place in society for a man like Meursault. The prosecutor then demands that the jury find Meursault guilty and sentence him to death.

The judge asks Meursault for a statement. Meursault is overwhelmed by the heat in the room and the prosecutor's grandiose statements. He tells the court that he never intended to kill the Arab. He says it was all "because of the sun," but no one understands what he means. Meursault realizes his explanation sounds ridiculous—he even hears a few people laughing in the courtroom—but he can think of nothing else to say.

Meursault's lawyer gives his closing argument the following day. As Meursault listens, he feels confused and detached, "worlds away" from the court and its proceedings. The lawyer never bothers to really discuss the crime, instead he goes into Meursault's personality and friendships, trying to portray him in a positive light.

During the speech, Meursault hears the bell of an ice cream truck out in the street. He recalls pleasant memories of his old life when he was free. Now he desires nothing more than to be able to go back to his cell and sleep.

Meursault awaits the verdict. He looks around the courtroom and sees all his friends. Marie waves to him, but he can't bear to wave back. Finally the verdict is read: Meursault is guilty. His lawyer assures him that he will get off with a few years sentence, but a while later, the judges come back to the room and announce that Meursault has been sentenced to death. The policeman gently leads Meursault out of the courtroom.

Analysis

Meursault finds himself becoming increasingly detached during the trial. The proceedings are so far removed from his own pattern of behavior that he finds them difficult to follow and even grows bored with them, despite the fact that he is on trial for murder and his life is at stake. Given Meursault's predilection for telling the truth as he sees it, his very participation in the trial would be a lie. He realizes that the purpose of the trial is not to arrive at the truth, but for one side or the other to win. The bombastic prosecutor and his own ineffectual defense attorney are like two combatants meeting each other in a public arena, fighting to win a contest. Meursault's sincere desire to tell the truth takes a back seat to the ritual of the trial. Once again, Meursault is unable to fit in, or understand, society's rules and conventions.

Commenting on his protagonist, Camus wrote in 1954, "L'Etranger is neither reality nor fantasy, I would rather see in it a myth incarnate in the flesh of the day's warmth. Many have wanted to see in it a new type of immoralist. That is entirely false. Meursault is not on the side of his judges, of social laws, of conformist sentiments. He exists, like a stone, or the wind, or the sea under the sun: none of them ever lies."

In Part One, Meursault's lack of emotion, dedication to routine, and simple enjoyment of nature seem to portray him as a "stranger," at odds with the world around him. However, once he is imprisoned and forced to confront other conventions, such as

the magistrate's rigid belief in God, and the trial itself, it appears that Meursault has managed to distance himself even further from the behavior and proprieties of a conventional society.

Some readers have suggested that Meursault killed the Arab in an attempt to shatter the odd routine of his life in the hope that it would lead him to a greater truth. Once he is behind bars, though, his alienation seems even greater and his behavior as enigmatic as ever. He even misses the few things that used to bring him pleasure. Although the misery he experiences from this sense of loss, along with his desperate circumstance, seems to be entirely self-inflicted, in the last pages of the novel, Meursault will arrive at a new understanding of himself and his place in the universe.

Study Questions

1. According to Meursault, what did the prosecutor "aim at" during his closing argument?

2. How does Meursault want to explain his lack of regret to the prosecutor?

3. What does the prosecutor call "the most odious of crimes?"

4. How does the prosecutor compare Meursault's crime to the parricide case?

5. Since Meursault has already admitted killing the Arab, what verdict does the prosecutor ask for?

6. How do some of the spectators in the courtroom react when Meursault tries to explain his reaction to the sun?

7. What word does Meursault's lawyer use when referring to Meursault during his speech?

8. What is Meursault's impression of his lawyer?

9. How is Meursault to be executed?

10. How do those near Meursault react to him after the sentence is read?

Answers

1. His purpose was to convince the jury that Meursault's crime was premeditated.

2. He wants to explain in a "quite friendly, almost affectionate way."

3. Parricide is called the "most odious of crimes."

4. He says Meursault is "morally guilty of his mother's death."

5. Murder without extenuating circumstances is the verdict he asks for.

6. They giggle.

7. He uses the word "I."

8. Meursault thinks his lawyer is inexperienced and less talented than the prosecutor.

9. Execution is by decapitation in "some public place."

10. They regard Meursault with looks of "almost respectful sympathy."

Suggested Essay Topics

1. Discuss how the prosecutor attempts to equate Meursault's crime of killing the Arab with the parricide case. Why?

2. Discuss how, during the trial, the emphasis shifts from an examination of the crime itself to a condemnation of Meursault's personality and behavior.

3. Do you think justice is served by the verdict? Can a man like Meursault, who is so at odds with society's conventions and morals, be given a fair trial? Is Meursault truly judged by a jury of his peers?

Chapter 5

New Character:

Chaplain: *a priest who talks to Meursault in his cell*

Summary

Meursault lies in his cell awaiting execution. He refuses to see the prison chaplain and he spends his time staring at the sky through his window. He fantasizes about escape, although he realizes that the possibility is highly unlikely. He wishes he had read more about executions and other escape attempts. He has difficulty accepting the finality of his situation.

Meursault recalls a story his mother once told him about his father. His father had attended an execution and had become "violently sick." At the time, Meursault says, he found his father's conduct "disgusting," but now he realizes that there could be nothing more important than an execution, and if he were ever free again, he would make it a point to attend every one he could. But Meursault realizes that he will never be free and he begins to shiver.

Meursault thinks of the guillotine. He concludes that what is wrong about it is that it affords the condemned man no hope at all that he might be spared. He thinks the laws and method of execution should be revised, so that the condemned might have some chance, even one in a thousand. Then he realizes that this is a ridiculous fantasy. He remembers seeing a photograph of a guillotine and recalls being surprised because the device was not on a platform but simply placed on the ground. He would prefer to climb up to it on a scaffold, a ritual that would capture his imagination. Positioning the guillotine on the ground carries with it, Meursault believes, "a hint of shame and much efficiency."

Meursault tells us that he stays awake all night, so that he will be ready for the executioners when they come for him at dawn. He does not know which dawn will be his last. He is forced to live every day as if it will be his last. He wonders if it makes any difference when you die, since we all have to die some time; but he is grateful for each day he is allowed to live. He also considers his appeal and the possibility that it will be successful. He understands that he must be prepared if the decision goes against him.

Meursault allows himself to think about Marie and to wonder why she hasn't written to him. He assumes she's grown tired of being the mistress of a condemned murderer. He wonders if she's sick or dead. He thinks he would forget about her if she were dead, just as he assumes others will forget him once he is executed.

The chaplain visits Meursault again, unannounced, and this time insists on seeing him. Meursault tells the chaplain he doesn't believe in God and has no interest in talking to him or in considering the question of God's existence. The chaplain says that other men in Meursault's position have eventually turned to God, and that, one day, everyone must face death. Meursault tells him that his situation is quite different from the average person who will eventually die.

The chaplain stands up and stares into Meursault's eyes, trying to intimidate him, but Meursault is not impressed. He tells us this is a trick he's seen other people use before. The chaplain demands to know if Meursault really believes there is no life after death. Meursault sticks to his position. He tells the chaplain that he is not aware of committing any sin, only being found guilty of a crime. The chaplain tells him that only God's justice is important. Meursault points out that it wasn't God who condemned him to die. He says he would rather not waste his final hours thinking about God and an afterlife.

The chaplain tells Meursault that he will pray for him and Meursault becomes very angry. He grabs the chaplain and yells at him, insisting that since everyone is condemned to death, it makes no difference how a person chooses to live. All people have been granted the same privilege of being alive, and they will all come to the same end, no matter who they are or what they have done during their lives.

The jailers rush into the cell to rescue the chaplain, who leaves Meursault's cell with tears in his eyes. Meursault is exhausted by his outburst, although he feels renewed. He falls asleep and wakes up several hours later. He hears the sounds of the countryside outside his cell, smells the earth, and enjoys the cool night air. He thinks about his mother and realizes that she must have

been happy at the time of her death because she was on the "brink of freedom." He believes no one in the world had any right to cry for her.

Meursault's angry tirade has left him at peace and ready to "start life all over again." He realizes that he had been happy and is "happy still." He makes no apologies for his life and tells us "I laid my heart open to the benign indifference of the universe." All that remains, he says, is that "there should be a huge crowd of spectators" at his execution and that they should greet him with "howls of execration."

Analysis

As he awaits his execution, Meursault fantasizes about the possibility of escape despite his belief that, ultimately, a person's life and death, including his own, is essentially meaningless. Death is inevitable so what difference does it make when or how he dies? Others will go on living after he is gone and he, like everyone, must die at some point anyway. He reminds himself that "life isn't worth living, anyhow." Nevertheless, Meursault finds he cannot "stomach the brutal certitude" of his death sentence, and he is angry at the society that has imposed the sentence and will carry it out.

Meursault finds the idea of life, even if it is lived in a prison cell, preferable to no life at all. Meursault's notion of a desirable afterlife, he tells the chaplain, is one where he can remember "this life on earth." Meursault chooses not to waste time thinking about the question of God's existence and hoping for a better life once he is dead; the matter simply doesn't interest him, and he has no time for it, especially now when he has so little time left. He only wants to experience the life he has on earth; something that is a certainty, at least for him. He insists on spending his time in the reality he is sure of, refusing to give away any of that precious time contemplating a complete unknown.

Meursault rages at the chaplain that the time Meursault has left, and his death, is far more vital than the chaplain's existence, which he compares to living "like a corpse." According to Meursault, the priest "couldn't even be sure of being alive." In dismissing the chaplain and his notion of God, Meursault is expressing his final rejection of society. Even in his last hours, Meursault is refusing to go along with the standard beliefs that most people turn to when they need consolation and comfort. Meursault also acknowledges the common bond between all people and the absurdity of their existence, knowing, as they all do, that one day they will eventually die. At this moment he is allowing himself to join with all human beings and their common dilemma: the awareness of their inevitable demise.

Meursault has struck out at society's conventions by refusing to mourn at his mother's funeral, by killing another man, and finally, by rejecting God. However, he has been honest to his own beliefs, and, in the end, is at peace with himself. His final act of rebellion is to wish that he will die hearing the screams and invectives of an outraged public. He has been true to himself and his convictions and in the end experiences a profound and peaceful awareness.

Study Questions

1. How many times has Meursault refused to see the chaplain?

2. The guillotine reminds Meursault of what other type of device?

3. How does Meursault spend his nights in his cell?

4. What subject does Meursault wish he had read more about?

5. What does Meursault do after he refuses to see the chaplain?

6. Instead of a "divine face," what image does Meursault try to see on the wall of his prison cell?

7. Does Meursault allow the chaplain to kiss him?

8. What happens when the chaplain touches Meursault's shoulder?

9. When the jailers rush into Meursault's cell, what do they do to him?

10. What does Meursault do after the chaplain leaves?

Answers

1. He refused to see the chaplain three times.

2. The guillotine's shining surfaces and finish remind Meursault of some type of laboratory equipment.

3. He forces himself to stay awake, waiting for the dawn.

4. Meursault wishes he had read more accounts of public executions.

5. He thinks about Marie.

6. Meursault tried to envision Marie's face, but he was never successful.

7. No, he does not allow the chaplain to kiss him.

8. Meursault grabs the chaplain and launches into an angry tirade.

9. They go to strike him but the chaplain begs them not to.

10. He falls into a deep sleep.

Suggested Essay Topics

1. Meursault states that he realizes that "nothing was more important than an execution." What do you think he means by this, and how does the story about his father relate to his present circumstance?

2. Why does the chaplain cry when he leaves Meursault's cell? Explain your answer.

3. Why would Meursault want to have a huge, angry crowd attend his execution?

Sample Analytical Paper Topics

Topic #1

Illustrate how Meursault's indifferent attitude and moral ambiguity is fundamentally at odds with society's expectations of how a person should think and behave.

Outline

I.   Thesis Statement: *In* The Stranger, *society views Meursault as a cold-hearted killer and a moral "blank." It categorizes him as dangerous and evil because Meursault refuses to conform to society's accepted standards of behavior.*

II.   Meursault's attitude and behavior

    A.   At his mother's vigil and the funeral

        1.   Meursault remains unemotional and detached

        2.   Doesn't want to see his mother's body

        3.   Drinks coffee and chats during the vigil

        4.   Offers no expression of comfort, or grief to his mother's close friend, Thomas Perez

        5.   Doesn't cry at the funeral

    B.   Relationship with Marie after the funeral

        1.   Marie's reaction to Meursault when she learns about his mother

2. Meursault's activities the day after his mother's funeral

    a. Swims with Marie

    b. Goes out on a date and begins an affair with Marie

C. Friendship with Raymond and agreement to write the letter

    1. Meursault never questions morality of writing such a letter

    2. Society's view of a man like Raymond and Meursault's association with him

D. Murder of the Arab and reasons for pulling the trigger

    1. Meursault shoots once, then fires four more times

    2. Meursault's bizarre explanation about "the sun"

E. No apparent remorse for crime

    1. Inability to ever feel regret about anything

F. Meursault doesn't believe in God

III. How society views Meursault

A. Behavior at the funeral is repugnant to many

B. Starts affair with Marie the day after the funeral

    1. Meursault enjoys himself, even though his mother has just died

C. Why is Meursault Raymond's friend?

    1. Raymond has a bad reputation

    2. Meursault must be involved with Raymond in some type of criminal activity

D. Why does Meursault murder the Arab?

    1. No one understands Meursault's explanation about the sun

    2. Must be part of suspected criminal activity

3. Meursault "murdered" his mother by putting her in a nursing home. His crime is even worse than the parricide case

4. Therefore, Meursault is capable of anything

E. Refusal to believe in God proof of Meursault's immorality

1. The magistrate's appeal to Meursault with the crucifix

2. Meursault's honesty interpreted as immorality

3. Meursault's rejection of the chaplain and everything he represents

IV. Meursault's understanding of himself and his actions

A. Alone in his cell, awaiting his execution, Meursault understands the significance of his behavior and crime

1. Final rejection of society and its attitude towards him

Topic #2

Discuss Meursault's reaction to the sun and its effect on his mood and behavior.

Outline

I. Thesis Statement: *Meursault behaves as if he were an element of nature, influenced by the sun, and not responsible for his actions.*

II. Meursault and the sun

A. Meursault reacts to the sun and heat at his mother's funeral

1. Reaction to sun supersedes other emotional reactions

2. This reaction misinterpreted by society which expects Meursault to behave in a conventional manner

B. Enjoying the sun with Marie while swimming

1. The sun as source of pleasure

2. Contrast to the heat and discomfort Meursault experienced on the bus and at the funeral

     C.   Running in the sun with Emmanuel to catch the truck

          1.   The sun blinding Meursault to everything but his most immediate desires, in this case, to catch the truck

     D.   Meursault, Marie, and the sun on the beach

          1.   The sun again supplying warmth and comfort

     E.   Meursault on the beach with the Arab

          1.   The heat and piercing sunlight conspire against Meursault

III. Destructive power of the sun

     A.   Meursault, estranged in the world, finds it impossible to relate to others in many situations when affected by the sunlight

          1.   Meursault on the bus to the nursing home

          2.   Sun influences his unusual behavior at the funeral

     B.   Blinding sunlight leads to his shooting the Arab

          1.   Moments leading up to the shooting

          2.   Meursault's decision not to go into the bungalow

          3.   The sun drives Meursault towards the cool stream and the fateful meeting with the Arab

          4.   The piercing sunlight in Meursault's eyes

          5.   The Arab's shiny knife

     C.   Heat and sunlight in the courtroom

          1.   Meursault unable to express himself to the judge and lawyers

     D.   Meursault's excuse about the sun is incomprehensible to everyone in the courtroom

IV. Meursault as an element of nature

     A.   Meursault living from moment to moment, influenced by the changes of nature

    B.   Meursault experiences no feelings of guilt or remorse

    C.   The sun as an indifferent force in nature, responsible for either pleasure or pain

    D.   Meursault's understanding of man's place in the universe

    E.   Contrast between Meursault's life and the existence of the sun

Topic #3

    The Stranger has been called an example of Camus' belief that "a novel is a philosophy put into images." Discuss how Camus' understanding of the absurd is depicted in *The Stranger*.

Outline

I.   Thesis Statement: *Meursault's actions and beliefs reflect the absurdist philosophy as understood by Camus.*

II.   Camus' definition of the absurd

    A.   Common personal experience of the absurd

        1.   Mechanical nature of individual lives

        2.   The inevitable passage of time

        3.   Human sense of alienation and isolation

        4.   Human beings' place in the universe

    B.   In literature and the arts

        1.   Other works by Camus including *The Myth of Sisyphus* and *Caligula*

        2.   Camus and the Theater of the Absurd

III.   Sense of the absurd as reflected in *The Stranger*

    A.   Meursault's routine life

        1.   His work and leisure time

        2.   How Meursault spends his Sunday

        3.   Encounter with the robot woman

B. Meursault's relationships

    1. His feelings for his mother, when she was alive and after her death

    2. Response to Marie's asking if he loves her

    3. Acceptance of Raymond as his friend

    4. Attitude towards, and treatment of, old Salamano

C. Life and death

    1. Meursault's reaction to the news of his mother's death

    2. Killing the Arab

    3. Contemplating his execution

    4. Meaning of life in the face of death

D. Benign indifference of the universe

    1. Nature as a representative of neither good nor evil

    2. The permanence of the universe and the images of nature

E. Meursault's acceptance of his own death and his understanding that all people are "condemned to die"

SECTION FIVE

Bibliography

Bree, Germaine. *Camus*. New Brunswick: Rutgers University Press, 1959.

Camus, Albert. *The Stranger*, Stuart Gilbert, trans. New York: Vintage Books, 1946.

Horne, Alistair. *A Savage War of Peace: Algeria—1954-1962*. New York: The Viking Press, 1977.

Lazere, Donald. *The Unique Creation of Albert Camus*. New Haven: Yale University Press, 1973

Quilliot, Roger. *The Sea and Prisons: A Commentary on the Life and Thought of Albert Camus*. University, Alabama: The University of Alabama Press, 1970.

Rhein, Phillip H. *Albert Camus*. New York: Twayne Publishers, Inc., 1969

Available at your local bookstore or order directly from us by sending in coupon below.

Available at your local bookstore or order directly from us by sending in coupon below.